Until Forever is Done

Copyright © 2020 by Gavin McDonald. All rights reserved.

No rights claimed for public domain material, all rights reserved. No parts of this publication may be reproduced, stored in any retrieval system, or transmitted in any form or by any means, electronic, mechanical, recording, or otherwise, without the prior written permission of the author. Violations may be subject to civil or criminal penalties.

ISBN:
978-1-63308-524-4 (hardback)
978-1-63308-525-1 (paperback)
978-1-63308-526-8 (ebook)

Cover and Interior Design by *R'tor John D. Maghuyop*
Illustrated by *Colleen Kelley*

CHALFANT ECKERT
PUBLISHING

1028 S Bishop Avenue, Dept. 178
Rolla, MO 65401

Printed in United States of America

Until Forever is Done

Gavin McDonald
Illustrated By: Colleen Kelley

Gavin:

For my girls, Kinley Marie and Maizey Kay.

Being your Daddy is my greatest pride, greatest accomplishment, greatest joy.

And for my Momma.

The love I have for my children was learned simply by watching you love us.

Colleen:

Thank you to everyone who has encouraged me over the years. To my loving family, my dear friends, and Gavin McDonald – this book is for all of you. Praise God for remembering this little girl's passion for drawing so many years ago.

"If there ever comes a day
When we can't be together,
Keep me in your heart,
I'll stay there forever."
—Winnie the Pooh

Looking down at his daughter, the love was intense

How could such a small thing provide joy so immense?

He'd finally done it, a Daddy at last!

The happiness inside could not be surpassed.

He was not perfect, he's messed up before,

But he knew from that moment he must be there for her.

So he made her this promise that night while she slept,

And a promise that big must always be kept.

Leaning into her crib, he kissed her goodnight,
And whispered these words as he turned out the light:
"I've said it before and I'll say it again,
I'll always be with you, from beginning to end."

Two years down the road, she was growing so fast

Her life mission was playing, and this she did best.

She cooked in her kitchen, she stacked up the blocks,

She changed tons of diapers, and threw tons of rocks.

One day while Daddy was on his computer,

His girl zipped by on her little red scooter.

But she was going too fast and the scooter did tip,

Sending her flying to the floor on her hip.

He quickly leaned down and pulled her up to her feet.
He placed her right back on the scooter's red seat.

Her eyes filled with fear as he knelt down behind her

And leaning in closely, whispered this small reminder:

"I've said it before and I'll say it again,

I'll always be with you from beginning to end."

Her shoes were brand new and her backpack was packed,

With pencils and paper and a lunch that's been sacked.

The first day of school had officially came,

She'd been practicing weeks on writing her name.

She held tight to his hand as the school bus came near

Her eyes became wide and her face filled with fear.

Would anyone like her? Would she know where to sit?

Would her teacher be mean? What if she gets hit?

She had so many questions, so much still unknown,

As she stepped on the bus she felt oh, so alone.

But her Daddy jumped on at the very last minute,
And cupping her ear whispered this softly in it:
"I've said it before and I'll say it again,
I'll always be with you from beginning to end."

Her car was gassed up and her bags were packed tight,
Graduation was over and her future was bright.
She stood in her room, all empty and bare,
Was she ready for this? Did she fully prepare?

College was waiting and a new life she'll start

And although she was ready there was still a small part

Of her heart that was nervous to leave all she's known

Without Daddy there, she would feel so alone.

She shut the car door and then put it in gear
Then drying her eyes put her hands to the wheel.

Then at the last second was a knock on the door,
Dad put in his head and assured her once more,
"I've said it before and I'll say it again,
I'll always be with you from beginning to end."

Looking at her, a gown sparkling and white,

He still saw the girl that fell off of her bike.

Time goes way too fast, now next to him stood

A beautiful woman stepping out of childhood.

His throat was burning and his eyes welled with tears

As he remembered his daughter through all of her years.

Glancing over to her he could see in her eyes

The fear in her face she was trying to disguise.

He squeezed her hand tight and leaned over to her

While her groom was approaching she heard him whisper:

"I've said it before and I'll say it again,

I'll always be with you, from beginning to end."

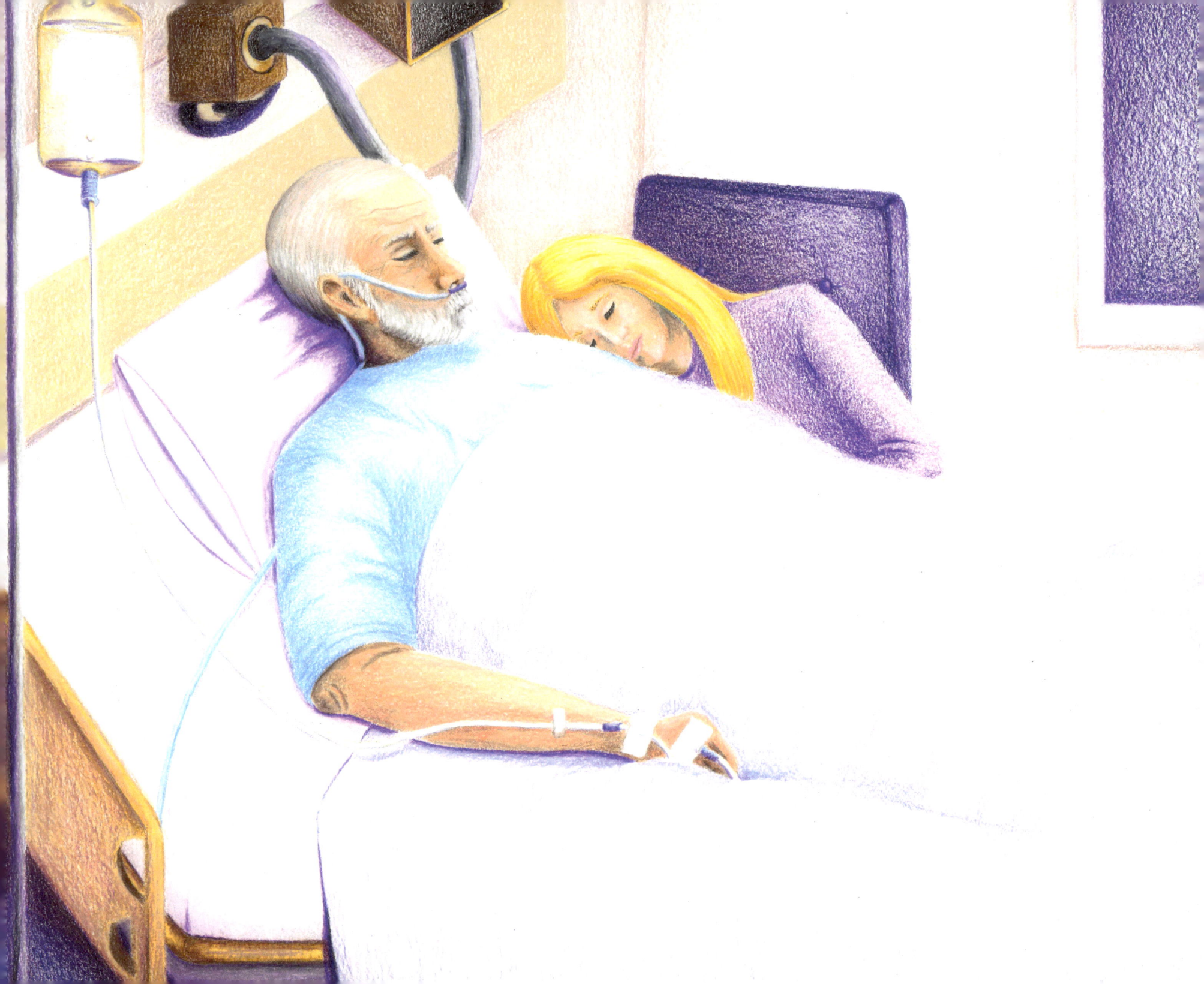

Looking up at her, he'd grown very old

He'd lived life completely, and fiercely, and bold.

He knew life was measured not by money or fame,

Not by titles or houses or by making a name.

It was measured so simply by love in his heart,
And the love for his daughter had been true from the start.
And the one thing he'd promised, to this he'd stayed true,

He'd loved her more deeply than deep can get to.

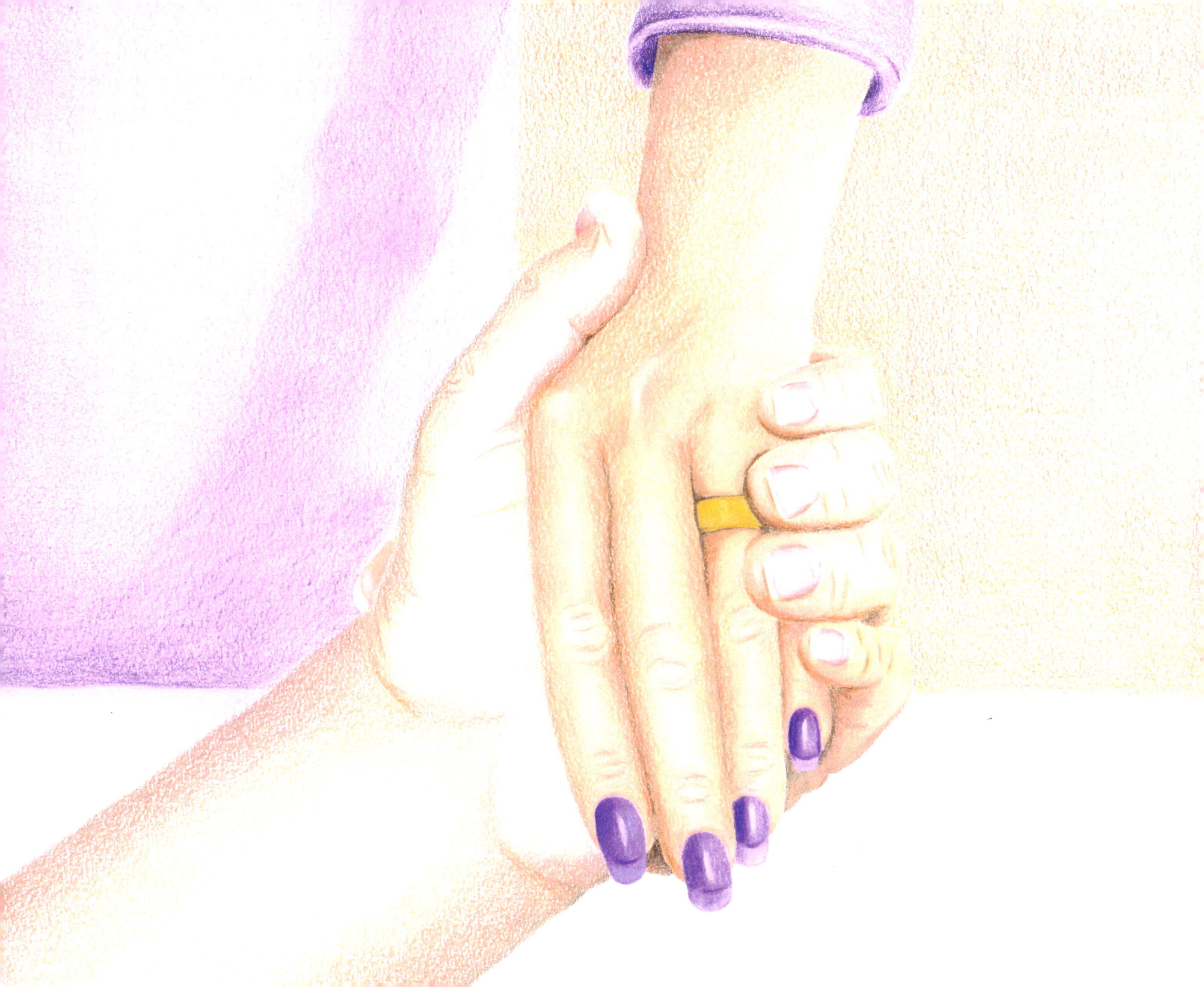

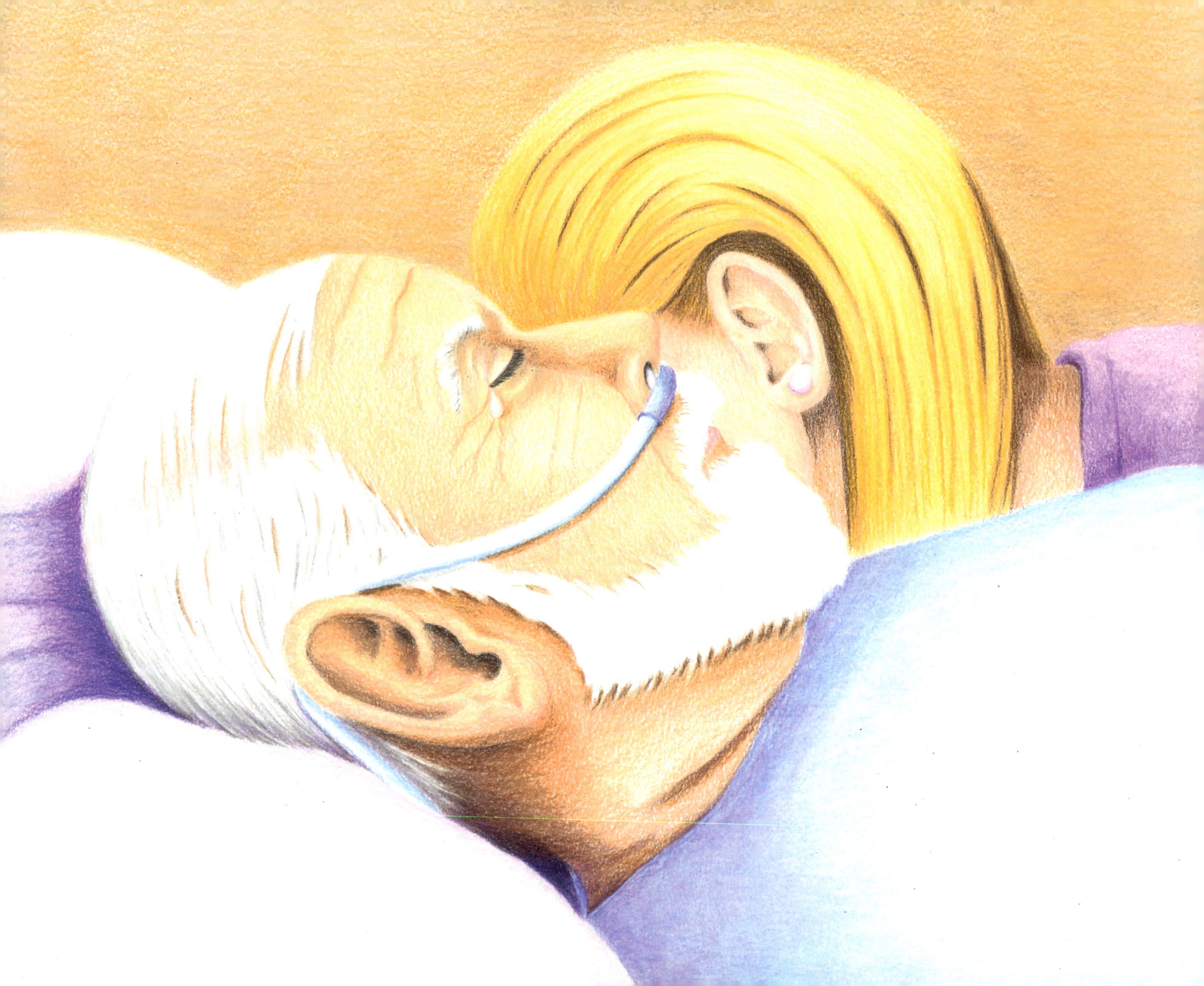

And pulling her close for one final time
Whispered gently to her his favorite rhyme:
"I've said it before and I'll say it again,
I'll always be with you from beginning to end.

If you remember my words and how much I loved you,
I'll be with you long after my life here is through."

Until the green trees refuse to grow leaves,

Until the cold snow refuses to freeze.

Until the tall mountains can fit in your hand,

Until the whole ocean is a desert of sand.

I'll be with you until one and one equals four,

When the waves stop crashing up onto the shore.

Until the cool Autumn shows up in the Spring,
Until all the birds forget how to sing.

I'll be here long after they turn out the sun.

I'll be with you forever, until forever is done.

Five years down the road, a new baby she holds

And the break in her heart at last was made whole.

She'll never forget the words that were said

To her long ago when Daddy put her to bed.

For when all is said, and when all is done,

She knew these words must be passed to her son.

Looking at him, big eyes bright and clear,

Leaning in close whispered this in his ear:

"I've said it before and I'll say it again,
I'll always be with you, from beginning to end…"

www.ingramcontent.com/pod-product-compliance
Lightning Source LLC
Chambersburg PA
CBHW041644070526
44586CB00004B/71